The Fears And Secret About Being Forced To Wearing A Dress As A Boy

By

Terry Virgil

Table of Context

Chapter One

Introduction to the beginning and just how it all began.

From Page 3 to Page 13

Chapter Two

The Conversion to Laurey Williams

From Page 14 to Page 26

Chapter Three

What Was It Like Putting On The Drees That I had To Wear On Stage.

From Page 27 to Page 35

Chapter Four

The Performance

From Page 36 to

Chapter one

Introduction

Why would I put these things in a book you may ask? Also why would a male like me even think about writing these things in a book for all to read in the very first place?

Here is the answer to the very first question that was asked in why I would put these things in my book for you to read.

In a lot of way in today's world fifty years after I was yes forced to wear a dress in matter of fact on stage is yes where we are going in answering the question why was I forced to wear well we are now going to say girls' clothing and you should try to understand that it has been over fifty years since that time period in my life time has passed.

Okay I was dressed as girl on stage in two different plays, but I can say I was dressed as a witch for Halloween party at school when I was in the first grade. Note: there was kindergarten was I was a young boy in my school back fifty years ago. So we are going to have to start from the first grade for me.

Now when I was a very young boy for some reason many people did mistake me as a girl a lot by the way, and this would include people that where friends of my parents, and even some of the friends I had as a very young boy, for even the girls that I knew did believe that I was a girl, for they even made comments like I should have bigger thighs as a girl, and a few other things too.

When I was a young boy I will tell you this much that yes I grew up in poverty and my parents even to this very date cannot read. We even lived out in the county, but on a farmer even though I did work on a farm to help in buying food and other things that we would need. I am also sure that I will give you some of my background history so that you could get an idea how I grew up and where I grew up, and the society that I was in back fifty years ago.

Okay back in the 1960's it was forbidden for a boy to even want to wear a dress or any girl's clothing at all, and it was very wrong unless like I did when I was in first grade for our class Halloween class party I was dressed as a witch.

Okay why did my parents dress me up as a witch for Halloween back in the 1960's one will never know and yes I do not even know why. So there your guess is as good and mine.

I should also tell you that even the school where I attending thought that I was a girl, for here is why.

On the very first day of school all of our names was printed on ether a blue for boys or on a pink for girls name card that was made out of construction paper. My name was put on a pink name card and I was mistaken as a girl in the first grade. Note this: I was mistake for a girl in grade school and yes I was forced into doing many things that a girl would have to do.

I was even told that I should be wear a dress like the rest of the girls would have to do in the 1960's, but they said see that I was living in poverty and they most likely thought that my parents was way too poor to even buy me a new dress or even dresses at all. So nothing was even said, but I can recall that I was told someday I should be wearing a dress. Okay the witches costume my mother made was the very first dress I ever wore. So for one day in first grade I was okay as a girl and my teacher I think accepted me as a girl and I was very sure she liked the fact that I was wearing a dress like a girl should.

Like I told you that many people thought that I was a girl, and yes I did pass a girl, but only by accident or people just thinking that I was a girl.

Okay my mother made my Halloween costume when I was in the first grade, and it was a

4

witches costume whereby I even now did pass as a girl for the first time that I could recall.

So just what is the big deal of me wear a witches costume to was by the way a home costume by my mother?

It truth not one thing was even wrong with me wearing a witches costume for a Halloween party at school. The other thing that was not wrong was the fact besides the Halloween party at school. A friend and I did go trick or treating, and I was wearing my witches costume with her too. So now you can see I did trick or treat as a witch and I did go with a friend of mine who was a female.

Let me get back to where my mother made my witches Halloween costume and kind of give you some idea what this she made and what she did in order to make me look like a witch. I can also tell you that in some ways my mother did teach me how to sit like a girl would, plus so pointer that I would need to know as if I was a girl in the first grade.

The fact was the skirt part of my witches costume was orange, and there was two parts to the upper part of the costume. I had on black tights, girls' panties and a girl's T-shirt or a training bra I am not sure while one it was, a pair of black girl's shoes. Mother even made the witches hat that I wore, but a neighbor lady help in making the wig that I wore. Mom did put black fingernail polish on me. She also put some makeup on me. She gave me a toy broom to carry. I almost forgot to say mom even showed me how to curtsey, and as I can recall she told me that I may have to do that.

Now it was very interesting that in first grade our teacher would have us take breaks in class and had to go to the bathroom, but I had just one problem that did happen before I would have to use the bathroom prior to the day of the Halloween party.

Seeing that my first grade teacher thought that I was a girl all the time and this did happen by the way. She always made me use the girls' bathroom always and she did make sure of that , for I got caught trying to use the boys bathroom just one time and she did not want me using the boys bathroom seeing that she thought that I was a girl, but things was a bit different that day and the days that would follow.

Here is a very strange thing that did happen out of all of that I was never pick on nor bullied, or even made fun of, for back then a boy would never even dare to wear a dress even a Halloween costume as a witch.

I can recall some of the upper class girl's state on the bus that we had to ride say it was about time I would wear a dress and be a girl like I was to be. Note: that I can recall one of them saying to me that I was a very purity girl and I should quit being a tomboy. I think she even told me to wear dresses even more, and if I need more dresses to wear she would give me some hand me down dresses and other clothing to wear. She even told me that I had to tuck the skirt part of the witches' dress that I had a little better, for a girl would do that. She believed that I did not know how that is why.

Okay I will confess that I did enjoy wearing the witches Halloween costume and I never told anybody that at all, for I felt not one person needs to know that at all. In today's world many would say great and it is good to show the female side in me, or they might think I am a transgender and I did not know it fifty years ago.

Now moving on from the Halloween party whereby I was dressed to look like a witch the problem of convincing others that I was not a girl was now a lot harder, for in first grade and the rest of my grade school years I just could not even do that, and yes I have several reason why I could not do that at all.

Note that it was first placed in my records that I was a girl, and it was also passed down to the other teacher that I would have that I was a girl and the label that was put on me was the fact that I was a tomboy and very tomboyish by the way. Our phy-ed teacher even made a point that I had to take girls' phy-ed and not to be part of the boys' phy-ed class at all.

The school nurse was even convinced that I was a girl, and she had me be a girl when it came to things of being a girl, for there was several times I had to report to the school nurse for things that is hard to explain yet even today.

In truth after the Halloween party in the first grade was the end of me even trying to be the boy that I am in grade school because things were passed down from one teacher to another made it even had for me to even use the bathroom of the gender that I was born with at the time of my birth. I even had to just forget about taking part in event at school as a boy and to take part as a girl.

I had one problem at school and my pants that I was wearing ripped the set out and my one teacher made me go to the principal's office so that she could fix my pants. Okay that may seem a bit strange to you but in my case as a boy who was passing as a girl, but when we got there she found a dress for me to wear and yes I had to wear it until she did fix my pants.

Seeing that I grew up in poverty and there was a time in which I did enjoy visiting my grandparent's house in the summer, for many reason why, but I can recall one summer that I had a surprise that maybe hard to believe. Now this would seem very unusable from a boy that was living in the 1960's and for a boy my age. In matter of fact my grandparent's had a neighbor that one would think is very impossible.

We'll let us get to just what did happen that summer at my grandparent's house and give you a picture of the times and yes how I was able to wear girls' clothing especially a dress with petticoats and other undergarments like a petticoat.

It all started with an invitation from the neighbor next door to my grandparent's whereby I was invited to go to a party, but here is a twist. Where I was invited to was for girls only. The party was a Strawberry Shortcake party whereby I would have to wear petticoats and white gloves etc... So I wore my very first Strawberry Shortcake type of dress.

Okay my grandmother came up with an idea that my shock you that she even bough me the type of clothing that made me looks like a girl and a Strawberry Shortcake type of girl.

I can recall grandma telling me that when it was time to get me ready for the party she told me to start by putting on the panties and white tights that she had bought for me, then to let her know that I had them on so that she could help me get the rest of the other Strawberry Shortcake type of clothing on, and I did just that.

Now because of that party I am very sure grandma came up with an idea that maybe it would be nice to have me wear a dress when it came to me helping her around the house dressed as a girl wearing address. Now she did her own homemade from scratch baking and cooking, do while I was wearing the dress she had given me to wear she would have me wear an apron made for girls to wear, and she had me go bare foot like I loved to do to help her hang the wash out side on the cloth line to dry. By the way I did learn how to cook and bake this way and to this date I still make my meals homemade from scratch just like my grandmother, and yes I also use what I learned from every great grandmothers as well. So yes even to this date I can thank my great grandmothers too.

Let me now move you to the fourth grade whereby again I was now forced to wear a dress on stage in a musical play that we were going to do.

The name of the play was HMS Pinafore, where this paly does take place in the Royal Navy with a love affair between a sailor and a female.

That all sounds okay, but there was a twist that I did not know back then and yes I did not even want to be in the play, but for some reason I was going to be in the play. I even landed the one leading role called Little Buttercup. Okay being a boy with a soprano singing voice and yes my music teacher even thought that I was a girl, and did force me to sing or to learn how to sing like a soprano girl would. I even did things to get out of even doing this, for one thing I did not even want to be on stage acting, and I surly did not even want to be on stage play the role of a female. The idea of even passing down the fact that some even thought of me being a girl and not the boy that I am. Did nothing at all, for again instead of fighting the fact that I should not have been given the role Little Butter cup I just accepted and was hoping this too would go away.

.The worst day in doing this play was the time when we were to receive our costumes that we were to wear in the play, for these were somewhat professionally made, by volunteers dress makers.

I was now measured and fitted for the dress that I was going to wear on stage as Little Buttercup. Even though it was a long dress I just did not feel very comfortable at first wearing a dress again, but in truth after the play was over I did enjoy wearing it too.

I should note that now I had another problem that did develop and now this time the boys in class even noticed that I was a very beautiful looking girl in the dress that I had to wear on stage. Even the girls in my class even made the comments that I was looking very beautiful as a girl even with the blonde wig that I was wearing even with the makeup om too. Both the boys and girls told me to quit being a tomboy and to be a regular girl. Yes my hair was just a lot longer than it is today, but it was down to my shoulders back then fifty years ago. In matter of

9

fact I was a blonde too in the fourth grade. Well I was a blonde hair male all my life, but my color has changed to a gray going on white now. I know that I should have told you easier.

Okay now that I had to wear a long dress in order to play the role of Little Buttercup in case you want to know about other female clothing that I wore. I wore yes panties and bra and white tights, with a slip, and some girls shoes that I had in a hand me down clothing that was passed down by other that thought that I was a girl. A note I would hide the female hand me down cloths from my parents.

My mother did keep the dress that I was wearing on stage when I played the role Little Buttercup in HMS Pinafore, plus she does still have some pictures of me wearing a dress dancing and singing on stage. Yes I did prove that I could play a female role in a musical play, and this will not be my last time I would play a female role in a musical play, for I did play Laurey Williams in the musical paly Oklahoma.

I would like to point out that yes two boys in the play and in my class did indeed did ask me to stay wearing a dress for they felt that I was a very beautiful girl. I even had about over half of the girls plus both my fourth grade school teacher and music teacher say and made a comment that I was a girl that should be wearing girls' cloth instead of being a tomboy, and the only reason why I had me wear a wig in the play was to get me to have a hair style that they knew would not work with my hair.

Now there was one thing that I was able to prove when I was Little Buttercup, playing a female role in the musical play is that I was a very fast learner, for most even thought that I was not a fast learner at all This would even be proven even more at a later date and time in my life. You will read about this when I was a fourteen year old boy, and at the age of fourteen it was more clear now people saw me as a boy instead of being a girl.

Now you could say this would be my last time in grade school whereby I had to wear a dress, but no that is not the case. Like I said when I was fourteen years old I would also have to wear a dress and dress up to look like a girl on stage, but there is more to that I will tell you later on.

In fifth grade I was forced to wear a dress and it was at this point I first began to try and say I am no girl and I was a boy, but to no avail. I got caught trying to use the boys' bathroom and my fifth grade teacher did remind me that as a girl I was forbidden to use the boys' bathroom, and demanded that I use the girls' bathroom from now on. She acted like I was trying to take a sneak peck to view boys. In my mind passing and having others think that I was a girl was over and yes I did try to resist every time but to no avail at first.

You the one and it was the biggest problem was that my first name was for girl's back in the 1960's and yes I was teased and yes picked on because of that and there was so many that thought that I was a girl even the boys and girls in my class. Being on stage as Little Buttercup in HMS Pinafore did not help matters to help me in my case to convince others even my teachers and principal that I was a boy. Okay my hair and the shape of my body even my height was a problem too.

Now yes when I had to go to the bathroom I would try to sneak in the boys bathroom or make sure that not one person saw me entering or exiting the boys bathroom or any boy even entering when I was in there at the same time. Let me put it this way trying to prove that I was a boy was so very hard that I almost gave up.

Okay I even did not even like learning about girl's health, for we had to learn about was the one thing that might been okay if I was a girl, well in matter of fact I did not even want to even learn about any health class issues or any health at all. Now why I am telling you this is the fact I got a break when I finely got a very small break in telling my teachers and principal that I was not a girl and I was a boy.

I finely got to tell some that all these years meaning every year I was not a girl came about when I got sent to the principal's office because I refused to use the girl's locker room to change for gym class, and this was the very first time relief for now came the end of the nightmare that was in my mind, and finely I start to end being shy and note that everything did go in the right direction and much better than I even thought, for even the surprise to everyone that I was a boy was great.

At first I was getting told that as a girl I had to change my cloth and shower with the other girls' is what all girls had to do and I should quit trying to say I was not a girl and I was a boy. Okay now here is how I finely got the chance to explain the fact that I was not a girl and by saying I will show you that I was never a girl and I want everyone to stop thinking that I am a girl. I said here I will show you. Then I pulled down my pants and underwear to show her my penis. I even told her I did not want to even do that I just wanted people to believe me.

This might have been a shock to her at first, but I can remember her words to me. I am so sorry that at this time we meaning my teachers and her thought that I was a girl and they did punish me to trying to say I was a boy and forcing me to do things that all girls would have to do and for being forced to be a girl when I was not a girl at all. She did remember me trying to tell her that I was a boy and she did not even want to hear about at all. She even saw the fact I tried, but no one would listen to me at all. Now seeing that even the principal did agree that I did try to tell everyone that I was a boy instead of a girl she did help me out by calling the teachers to her office and explained that a mistake was made with me and told them the next time to listen to me when I was trying to tell them the I was a boy instead.

Now after that day things did change for the good until I was fourteen years old and this time I did not have to prove that I was a boy, but this time I had to play another female role in our school play that I did not even want to be in at all. Now everything will be told in a later time in this book too.

Chapter Two

The Conversion to Laurey Williams

Here is my point in 1968 it was forbidden for a boy to wear female clothing, and in 2016 many are protesting against the moral values of a male of a man not wearing female clothing. another words people are saying it is okay for a male to wear female clothing. There are also people in 2016 even say that they are very glad to see a boy wearing girls' clothing and acting like a girl. They also say in 2016 that a boy should be able to use the girls' bathroom, locker room, and changing room whenever they feel like it without any recourse or any legal action even taken out against them for doing so. People even in 2016 say the very same thing as if a girl was a boy as well. In matter of fact people say an adult male should wear female clothing and to be able to use the ladies bathroom, locker room, or changing room and the very same things go for female would want to wear clothing for male to wear too. So reverse gender roles are what people of 2016 want us human beings to do.

Now why was I forced to wear a dress in 1968 as a fourteen year old boy and a very shy boy in matter of fact? You could ask what was it that I said and did that caused and why I was forced to wear a dress and dress up a female in 1968. Now why was I forced? Yes the word force is here and for a very good reason why.

Now how did I become so very shy while I was dressed as a younger boy or even mistaken as a girl while I was in grade school is why I was in a shell in the very first place, for I did not even want to have any more that I was a boy who was forced to wear girls' clothing and even put in a school play dressed as a girl on stage. It was this event that caused me to be shy. Yes some of my classmate knew this, but things seemed to get better and those events have gone away when I was fourteen years old. I even had a friend that knew that I was mistaken for a girl when I was in grade school who did keep very quit and she did help me in an event that did happen to me at the age of fourteen to help me do a great job when again I had to be on stage playing a female leading role, also with the help of the boy that got the leading male role in the same play too. So this time I had support and lot of help to get past this as well. Yet this time things are different as well.

In truth as a fourteen year old boy in 1968 I would have to agree that is was very morally wrong of those that did force me to wear a dress as part of my punishment. Yet I did have some flash back to what it was like in grade school trying to convince people that I was a boy and not a girl, and now I had to play a female role again. Just think what was going on my mind at that time as a fourteen year old boy now forced to do this again. The real fact is that I was not allowed to even express what I wanted to say about in Shakespeare's day that it was okay that women cannot play female role or even be on stage in a play, and the fact that men had to play female role was fine in Shakespeare's day but in 1968 it is not even okay for a boy to even wear any female clothing even on stage.

Now you know I was punished for a comment that I made about why males had to play all roles in plays during the time of Shakespeare's day, and why females could not even be in any play in order to act. Keep this in mind as well that I was forced to be in drama class as well in 1968 and this fact is truth that I did not even want to be in any drama class at all. I want to take up shop and yes I was very upset at the time for even being forced into drama class where I did not want to even take as a course at all. You see even back in 1968 I felt that a person should not be forced in to doing something against their will like all liberals and feminist would like to have us do. Even all the one that are or claim to work in the mental health field want to force a male or in my case today to dress like a female, even in a drama class where a boy like me was only fourteen years old.

You see back in 1968 the liberal feminist movement was getting bigger and getting more out of control. Just like it is today in 2016, for the feminist movement has gotten so out of control that it is hard for a male to even say no to the liberal feminist at all. The fact is in 2016 the very liberal feminist organizations and groups today want to see and have all males be very famine to include and require that all boys wear female clothing even to the point whereby a boy is to wear a dress. This would include the fact that they would like to see every male share the very same bathroom with females, and end the separation of bathrooms, changing room, and locker rooms. The very same thing they want and demand to have it a mandate that even females are to be allowed into men's bathrooms, locker rooms and even changing rooms too. This is called gender equality to be equal in the name of equal right[s] for all. Now even if I would of said no to a liberal feminist I would even be punished worst because it would be consider as a non-politically correct thing, and The very liberal feminist would even say I have no tolerance at all.

Here is my comment that I did make in 1968 and it is not bad at all. I said something like this. That it is good that male cannot play a female role in a play now days because we have females to play all the female roles and parts in a play and male must not and should never play any female or a male should never wear any female clothing at all. Or words to that effect or something like those words. I even remember saying that a male would look very funny wearing a dress and other types of female clothing too; therefore you would never see me wear a dress or any other type of female clothing. Well that did not go very well with my very liberal feminist drama teacher and very well with my very liberal feminist principal too. It was for this reason why I was both forced and punished in a very different way.

I was almost expelled in 1968 for just saying those words, but the idea of even expelling a good student was not a good idea for my very liberal feminist principal to do. Instead of expelling from school and the fact that as a drama class we were going to do the musical play Oklahoma by composer Richard Rodgers and librettist Oscar Hammerstein II whereby I did not even want to be in the play either. If I was to be or take part in the play I wanted to be in the back ground. My very liberal feminist drama teacher came up with this idea and passed it along to my very liberal feminist principal too as punishment instead of expelling me from school.

The idea was I was to play the leading role in the musical play not as a male, but have me play the female leading role Laurey Williams. Is okay in 2016 this would not be too bad and just was the big deal of having me play a female role back in 1968, for I was just a very shy boy. Now in 1968 a boy would have any problems even for just thinking about even wearing a dress and dressing up to look like a female. Okay you may be thinking that I would have to just be on stage as a male pretending to be a female, but while in class I had to be a female and learn how to be a female as well.

Now my very liberal feminist drama teacher and very liberal feminist principal came up with an idea that would help me out overcome being bullied, teased, and pick on. Yet I still had just one problem that was in fact addressed later in school. It would be my grade for that class and project.

If you would happen of read my first two book " How I played Laurey Williams in 1968, for I was a shy boy back then" and " How I played Laurey Williams in 1968, for I was a shy boy back then part 2" you would see that I did it and was successful in playing the role Laurey

Williams in the musical play Oklahoma. You would even to get to see some of the dresses that I had to wear in the play and somewhat what I had to go through doing that play and being Laurey Williams too.

Yes even though I was against this idea about me now being forced to wear dress and to play the role Laurey Williams in the musical play Oklahoma and so was my parents. As you know I did agree to do this and so did my parents and it had nothing to do with my grade and yes I got an A+ for my performance, it was this reason why I did it. I felt back in 1968 that yes a boy should not even wear a dress based on Deuteronomy 22:5 " A woman must not wear men's clothing, nor a man wear women's clothing, for the LORD your God detests anyone who does this." Yes this was one of the things that I said and referred to when I spoke up to state a male must never wear a dress or to even look like a female. It was this statement that got my very liberal feminist drama teacher got angry about. This also why I was told I am going to play the leading role Laurey Williams and this would be the only way I could stay in school. Now you can see that in truth that Laurey Williams is just the opposite of me in personality, for she was not shy and I am shy or was shy at the time. The major difference was I am a male and Laurey Williams is a female.

In the case you the reader is wandering why the very liberal feminist drama taught come up with this idea that I was to play the role Laurey Williams in order to stay in school and in class is to show that yes a male can still play a female role and that Idea was not over because it was 1968. She felt that it would be very good for a boy not just to even play a minor female role, but she thought that a male should play a leading role and I was the one picked to do just that. Let put it this way force is the correct word to use, and please note this that I did my share of resistance too in a way. Yes I was very careful how I did my resistance, but I did do that throughout the whole production. Even if it did not seen like I was even resisting at all. I was in truth every day and every moment.

My time I did resist was the day I was taken to a room in school was to get measured for my costumes and to what I was to even wear as undergarments. Wellbeing fitted to the type of undergarments that was worn in 1906 by ladies even girls of that time period is hard for women today and even in 1968 was hard to do or deal with. A male doing this was even harder, but for me I was being forced to do something that no boy that was 14 years old and is a very shy boy to do was even harder yet. I even believed that a boy should never ever wear any female clothing no matter what.

I had to adjust to the point that I would resist in my mind, but not show that I was resisting at all. A good example I would resist by sitting with my arms cross while I was being measured for the size of the dresses that I was to wear. I would even try to forget lines and movement, but to no avail. By the way the lady that made the costumes that I was to wear was from the local Preforming Arts Group so she had a very good idea on just what types of dress to make for me to wear. Note that the local Preforming Arts Group was doing the exact play too, so some of the dress that they had that was not being used our class was to use in our production. Well you get the idea of the costumes and the makeup came from and just who helped apply the makeup we were to use and have on.

Let us go back to where the class was told all about this and yes there was some being . picked on and teased, but there was a thing that did come up whereby I was not to be teased, bullied, or anything as such. In truth what was laid out and how things were going to go the boys did not tease me, for I had a few say they had a fear that they would have to play a female role too. Now the girls in class did tease me just a little bit, but that was not too bad. I was able to get over it. Now I remember the girl that wanted to play Laurey Williams in the play and yes she was jealous at first, but after she landed the role Aunt Eller in the play she told me that she liked that part even more. She also told me that she would help me learn how to be a female and the role of Laurey Williams.

At first I was told that I would have to put a dress on just in class only just for readings and rehearsals. Yet there was a problem[s] that came about for I would just wear the clothing that a boy would wear under the dress that I would use for readings and rehearsals. Which did not work and was one of the things I would do just to rebel or resist against the idea of being the leading female role in the play or even wearing a dress to look like a female.

Okay the idea I had of wear my boys' cloth under the dress that I was to wear did not work out because after the very first day of doing this I was reminded of staying in school and my grade. So on day two you guessed I had the dress on and this time I was baring my legs for the very first time.

Now let me try to describe to you just how I looked in 1968, and one of the reasons why I was forced to play a female role and it was the fact that I had not yet develop as a boy would, for I was told I looked like a girl from time to time in my past from others. In matter of fact even some of the boys even thought that I was a girl along with the girls. I even did pass as a girl one time when we took a vacation trip, and note my parents did not say anything for I remember them saying that it was funny that I just pasted for a girl. There was a lady that lived next door to us even though that I was a girl. Now I think that you the reader have some idea just how I looked like a girl at the age of fourteen, but I am a boy. In truth I did not like the idea that people though I was a girl even with my hair style was a one that a boy would have.

According to what was said after 1968 about me playing the role of Laurey Williams I had no idea just how much people like my very liberal feminist drama teacher love the idea that our very liberal feminist principal had in forcing me to play the role of Laurey Williams. Yes I met them in my past from time to time. Well I even met some of my fellow classmates too that where in the play from 1968. My very liberal feminist drama teacher did state to me that was a very great idea and she was not even sure at the time that it would work out at all. See said I made a great Laurey.

Okay seeing that everything was going at a very fast pace and I would have not just learn my lines and that was one of the things going through my mind at the time, but the other problem how any I going to be a good and convincing Laurey, but just how I was going pass as a girl too.

Learning the lines was not hard for me to do for I could memorize lines very fast and easy. In truth many did not know this one thing about me. The hardest thing for me was how to be a female or a girl in this case. Well a fourteen year old girl to be exact. The other problem and this was not the biggest problem was wearing female clothing, for I had no idea on just how to do that unless I would observe just how a female walks and moves while wearing a dress or even a skirt.

This may sound like it was hard for me to even observe the way a female moves and wears a dress, but one other problem came up too. I would have to learn how to dance and walk like a lady.

Being shy is the reason why it was very hard for me to observe just how a female would be when she is wearing a dress. In truth I would have to learn how to try and be a female while I was wearing a dress. It was one thing observing not wearing a dress but observing while wearing a dress, for I got to learn how to imitate a female much easier. Yet there was one problem at first. I was and would wear the boy's clothing that I had one and with a dress over my clothing mad it even hard for me to move because it got much tighter and binding where the female movements that I had to learn was harder for me to do.

Even if I knew that I would have to do this my very liberal drama teacher made this point to me that I should learn how to move and wear a dress like a lady. Well who knew we were on the very same page in that category . She even had any idea that did help me learn those things and in truth I was not sure about it at all.

The idea was that I would wear a dress during class and at all readings and rehearsals and no boy's clothing under the dress that I was to wear in class. Then this idea came to her as well that I would have to wear a bra, and panties with tights and girls shoe that would fit me until I got the female western boots that I was to wear in the play. While I was doing this wearing a dress I would learn how to move like a lady very fast. Example I learned how to sit, walk, dance, and even be more famine than I realized. In truth I even did these entire thing in my own natural way, for moving like a male would was not natural to me because I was trying to be female.

Now what about me wear a dress without the wig I was to wear in the play you may ask? The answer is simple I was in fact wearing a wig all the time and it was the very same wig I wore in the play. I would even say the wig did help me learn how to be a lady too.

Every classmate did want a good grade like we were told, and some of the girls in class did help especially the girl that did want to play Laurey, but ended up playing Aunt Eller took me to the side to help me learn how to be a lady. Believe me this was a hard task, but in truth this worked, and we were able to learn our lines faster as well then some of the rest. This other fact was she was my next door neighbor so we even work on this problem on the weekend.

I could recall that the girlfriend even told me that she could see me playing the role of

Laurey Williams in the play if I kept my mind on being a lady more, for Laurey was coming out of very we will say more natural than she even expected. This she even did was to teach me how to cross my legs like a lady, and yes for a boy this would be hard to do is you was not the size of a boy that I was in 1968, but this would help me pass as a girl and help in the playing of Laurey Williams too. She even told me that it was very important that I would not be so shy and get over the fact that I was to play the role of Laurey Williams in the musical play Oklahoma, and said if I recall correctly that I should just get over it and be a female in class and quit worrying about it. She even gave me some clothes to wear as well. Just dresses and some skirts only no undergarments. These cloths my girlfriend gave me to wear was we can say was training tools that help her teach me how to be Laurey Williams, for she was Aunt Eller and she even said this does make it even easier for her to learn her part and lines too.

Let me go bad to this one event as we are introducing you to me being forced to play the role Laurey Williams is this one fact that the next day when I got to school I did not think this would happen to me, but as you can see I did whatever I could to even disrupt the production of the play, but there was one thing that was hard for me to do at first and now it would be time to cover that one thing that did happen to me.

The next day I was called to the principal's office to meet with my very liberal feminist drama teacher and very liberal feminist school principal. Here are some of the things that did happen to me in this meeting with the very two very liberal feminist principal and drama teacher was the fact that the night before my very liberal feminist made a phone call to the local preforming arts group in our town and asked if she could get some help turning me into a girl then into Laurey William. She asked to bring some dresses and some other clothing even undergarments that a girl of 1968 would wear and anything else that they felt would help me learn and how I would become a girl.

Okay besides me meeting with my very liberal feminist drama teacher and very liberal feminist principal I had to meet with two makeup artist, and two costume designers, and they had me first change into girls' undergarments such as panties and a training bra then had me wear a slip, tights, a dress then try on different types of shoes to wear. All of that was to have me learn and get use to wearing female clothing. Okay as I can recall I spent around two to three hours in that private room in my very liberal feminist principal's office with these ladies trying on different clothing for a fourteen year old girl at first then getting my face makeup to make me look like a fourteen year old girl with trying to find a wig that would both look nice on me, but to make me look like a fourteen year old girl in 1968. Yet there was an idea that I cannot remember who came up with it, but I can recall that I should learn to wear girls' clothing that was of that time period, but I must learn how to be a female.

In today's secular, very liberal worldview this would be great to do too was to have me wear girls' clothing not just to teach me a lesion, but to teach me that it is okay for a boy to wear girls' cloth and to be a feminist type of boy. In truth I would have been classified as a transgender in today's secular, very liberal worldview. That is the new norm as it goes with the worldview in 2016 that a boy must be allowed or even forced to do these things, and it would be acceptable however we are talking about 1968 whereby these types of things was not acceptable and should have been forbidden. Civil Rights and the ACLU would say this to me that I must wear girls' clothing not just for the time I was in drama class, but also for the rest of my life. This is just like what is being told as of a secular very liberal worldview, for the ACLU and those liberal demanding Civil Rights are saying that a boy must and will have to wear girls' clothing all the time.

This was on my mind as I was forced to wear girls' clothing and I did not say anything to one person until today.

After trying on the very first dress and the girls' undergarments that I had to wear in class for others to get use to the idea of having me just wear a dress and play the role of Laurey Williams was that I was very embarrassed to the point of running away. I did not even want to be classified as a homosexual or gay type of boy, for I was not at all. I did not even want to be called or classified as a girl. I was called a girl a few times like I feared, but I did just over looked those things. I did not even want to be forced to act like a lady or be told that I must do things like a girl. These were a few things that were on my mind in 1968.

Okay after I put on my very first pair of tights in order to cover my legs did give me a feeling that I was now going to have to accept a fact that when the very first slip and dress was put on me was now this is going to be real and there was no way I could get out of the fact I was going to be playing the role of Laurey Williams at that was it. Seeing the dress on me and seeing the very first wig being placed on my head then having the very first time I would wear makeup I knew from that point on I would have to change my voice to be a female voice and do this on a daily bases.

Here is one thing that was or could be very interesting about the very first time I was wearing a bra. Now to a girl this is to be very normal thing to do, but for a boy it was not a normal thing to do. Girls even dream of the day were they will be wearing a bra, and the lacy part and designs that make a bra to be very appealing to them to wear. With me this was not the idea for me to do. Okay I would not of been even having a desire to wear a bra, but now that I was forced to I can say I was not ever very comfortable and I wanted to just cry. Okay the fact that I would not have any breast development at all a makeup artist did make false breast for me to wear that would be about the size I would have been at the age of fourteen if I was a girl. Yes the false breasts were glued in place to have then from in the right place. These breasts were as natural looking as possible.

I thought that I would be trying on the girls' clothing and dresses in the principal's office only, but no that was not the plan at all. I was escorted to class by all those that made me up to look like a girl and that would even include my very liberal feminist drama teacher and very liberal feminist principal too. While I was being escorted to class I was even told if I had to go to the bath room a teacher or an adult female would have to escort me to the girls' bath room so that I would have privacy and be protected as well. Yes the very first time I left that room in my principal's office was the most scariest one of all. I was even afraid to even walk out, for I was even afraid of be started at in which I was at first, but I had a fear for I had to go to the bath room at first. Yes it was my very liberal drama teacher that took me to the girls' bath room and notes this was my very first time in the girls' bath room. I was very reluctant to go at first. Yet I did it. Thank fully there was no girl in that bath room.

Let me put it this way there is more that I could tell you the reader of this book in the introduction and first chapter of this book, but let's look at it this way you have some good idea of what was on my mind and what I was going through in 1968 be forced to yes play the role of Laurey Williams, but to also be forced to be a girl at the same time when I was just a fourteen year old boy in 1968. I also feel it is time to now move to chapter two.

Chapter Three

What Was It Like Putting On The Drees That I had To Wear On Stage.

The conversion from a very shy boy to a girl is a question that one could ask just to see how hard it was for me to do. Okay in truth I am and was a very good learner and a good listener, for that is how I am about to learn many and different things. Even how to convert from a very shy boy to a girl.

Now as you read from chapter one the introduction was designed to give you some idea just how and maybe not in a chronological order of things that did take place for it would be hard to place since it has been over forty-eight years since this took place.

As a very shy boy I would not even want to even deal with anything like or even be in a play even a musical play or sing in public or preform on any stage, yet I had to do this thing that I happen to disagree with in the very first place. So converting from boy to girl was hard to do.

Okay from a very shy boy to girl took place the next day when I gotten to school after it was explained to me and my parents the purpose of me being in the play in the very first place and the events that led up to that moment.

Getting called to the principal's office was the very first thing that took place in order to convert me from a very shy boy to a girl. The second step was getting the right people to assist in make and finding costumes and girls' clothing that would fit, and explaining to me what I had to get use to wearing and why I was to wear it.

The other part was to have me wear a bra and to get fitted to that type of bra and to find the right breasts that were needed to have me wear in the bra I was to wear to make me look like a girl that would be at the age of fourteen year old girl in 1968.

You may ask why was a bra and me having breast that would be for a fourteen year old girl was so important well the answer is this that in order to make me look like a fourteen year old girl, for it was this idea and the only way I could even pass as a girl in the first place; plus I would be a more convincing lady in the play.

It would hide the fact I was a boy and not a girl. Yes having me wear a bra with fake breasts this trick did work by the way, even some of my classmates forgot that I was a boy.

There is one other point that should be made here as well is the fact that I was being punished, and there is even more to the punishment that I have told you so far. You can also see why I would be very nervous in doing this too. This time the punishment was more than being on stage a girl this time again, it goes even more too where yes I had to even do it not just for my grade, but for the whole class too. This would become a class project too and a major class project too. The thing is we are going to talk more about the playing of the role Laurey Williams in the musical play Oklahoma.

Okay the bra was not the only piece of the undergarments that I would have to wear, for I had to wear panties and tights along with a slip, for back in 1968 girls did wear slips under their dresses or skirts too. Please note I was not at all very comfortable even wearing these things and that would go with even wearing a dress too.

So you can see that the events in the principal's office was the very first step in order to convert me from a very shy boy to a girl. Then I would have to even be converted from a girl to Laurey Williams too.

While being forced to wear girls' clothing on the first day I was forced to do that. I was also even measured for the costumes that I was going to have to wear on stage when I became Laurey Williams too. Now the style of clothing was for a woman to wear in 1906 back when Oklahoma was just a territory and about to become a State in the Union.

There was thing that I was measured for and I had several fittings for this part of my costume was the western style not too high of a heel female boots that I had to wear on stage. Note: these are the very first time I even had to wear any high heel footwear of any sort. The high heel was I am going to say was about two inches, and yes I knew that even back then all females did have a hard time walking in high heels first. So this was the very first thing I had to get use to wearing and walking in. I would have to learn how to dance in those very same high heels too. So this was very new for me to do, and interesting too. Yes I did master the art of wearing high heels when they were done; I even had no problems what so ever.

A wig was found for me to wear that did match my natural hair color which was a blondish hair color, but mine would be more of a blondish brown as my natural hair color. The wig was a reddish blonde that was longer for it was just past my shoulders in leigh.

Before I had to leave the room in the principal's office wearing the dress that I was forced to wear so that I could now learn how to be a girl then latter on become Laurey Williams I had to now learn how to walk, sit, standing like a lady or a girl would in the first place. None of this I had to do when I was first forced to wear a dress or even be on stage as Little Buttercup, so now learning something new. They even wanted me to learn and to develop a girl's speaking voice to use as well.

Okay my size and body shape was not even what one would expect a fourteen year old boy would have, for I did not even develop into what a male would do in puberty at all. I still had a soprano singing voice and a somewhat high pitched voice as a boy in 1968 at the age of fourteen. I am very sure you have a good idea about me at the age of fourteen.

Now for the most horrifying moment in my whole life and the most embarrassing part of everything too. I was told that as part of my punishment I had to be in that class dressed as a girl so that I would get use to wearing a dress and to sit, stand and walk like a female would. The other thing I had to do and yes I always had to have a female teacher or an adult with me every time I had to go to the bathroom dressed as a girl for protection, and to make sure it was safe for me to go and use. There was one thing not one knew that I was use to using the girls' bathroom in the first place, and I did not tell them this, for I just wanted them to think this was my very first time even being a girl or passing as a girl, so using the girl's bathroom was not new to me as I told you in chapter one.

The one thing and a real fact was that I had to be convinced that I could become a girl again and to be able to play the role Laurey Williams. Which was the very last thing I wanted to do even at the age of fourteen. This would not be hard for me to do because if you recall I had to do this in grade school. Secondly I did not even want to be on stage at all, but converting for me to do this was not a problem, but those thinking that I never did this did not know that I did these things, for they did from time to time wonder why I was able to adapt to being a girl and now being on stage as Laurey Williams.

Let look at this problem that I had to overcome and yes we can say it was the first problem, but in truth once I did overcome some other problems that I had to learn was I had to learn who to walk like a lady should by keeping my legs together and gliding just a little bit. Another words I would have to learn how to sway my hips while walking. Now by doing this I would be able to sit and dance like a lady would. Even keeping my legs together while walking like a lady even helped me learn how to cross my legs when I had to sit down like a lady.

Now after one week after getting measured from the female western white high hell boots that I was to wear even helped me more how to keep my legs together so that I could walk like a lady does. I even found out that the boots where very comfortable to wear, but my very liberal feminist drama teacher with the help the other ladies that were helping out in the play and us students learn our roles did notice that while I was wearing the boots did help me even more to learn how to be a female and even how to be Laurey Williams at the same time. By the way I had no trouble even walking in those boots like many would think I would.

Now time to be on stage and to wear the costumes that I was to wear on stage and get use to wearing them and to yes be real comfortable wearing these dresses on stage.

The reason why this time being on stage was that us as a class had to now learn about the whole production of a play more than just getting our parts and rehearsing our lines. We had to learn all about the characters, plot, theme, songs, and movements like where to stand and how to dance, direction, music, and spectacle which are the parts in the production of a play. I had to learn all about Laurey Williams how much she was different than I was, for I had to learn not to be shy, for she was bolder. Another words I had to put myself into her character and in truth become her. This is what we had to learn in drama class, plus that is why this is a class project to in truth become the role that we were given to portray on stage. This is the main reason to have me wear dresses and to apply makeup on before both dress rehearsals and the opening night on stage in our characters.

I had just only one problem learning the character of just what Laurey Willems was like and now wear female clothing style from 1906 and what it was like living in the Oklahoma territory.

Everyone should know by now from my past history I ether passed as a girl or was dressed to look like a girl even on stage. Okay why is this different and I did tell you it was for a grade and was part of a class project, plus there was my classmates counting on me preforming not just well, but great. So the pressure was now on.

Okay the very first time I put on bloomers and a chemise, corset, petticoats, garters, along with the tights on was not very comfortable at all for me to wear. Now the bloomers to me was like wearing knee high pants but loose feeling. The chemise was like wearing a slip, but the corset worn properly was tight and uncomfortable at first, and note I did enjoy wearing this because I was able to move more like a lady from 1906 would, and it gave me more a female way of moving even when I had to dance too. Now this may seem very strange to say wearing a corset did help me feel like a proper lady of 1906. The corset even gave me the proper breast size that was needed, but there was later added fake breast that would be the size that would be if I was a fourteen year old girl. There was even talk of me wearing a bra with the proper cup size as part of my costume on stage, but that did not happen. The corset and fake breast was enough and that was good.

The girls in class did help me in learning how to be a lady and we did rehears a lot so that we can get this production off to a good note, plus so that we could get a good grade too. They even well had me become one of girls and allow me to partake in being a female in how to walk, sit, talk, sing, move, and dance just like a lady would. So now everyone was part of my learning and their learn process in doing and helping me convert from a very shy boy to Laurey Williams and to get even more comfortable wearing a dress on stage. Was it easy? Well sometimes yes and sometimes no. By the way the girls in class just accepted me as one of them after about the first two weeks.

Now beside our very liberal feminist drama teacher teaching our class she had the local

Preforming Act Group help teach us that were in the drama class learn our lines and movements. Now there was one thing that we learned that year was the fact they were also preforming the very same musical play too. I even met the lady that was doing the very same role as I was and it was her that got me to convert and to be more comfortable playing the role Laurey Williams too. I learned how to wear the dresses and the undergarments much better, plus she found out that I was a very quick and good learner too. She even told me that she loved the way I was preforming on stage and I was a natural too.

The lady that did the makeup for the girl and this would even include me was the one who taught me how to smile more like a lady would and how my face expression should be.

It would be the wardrobe lady and costume designer that was the one who showed me how to do thing like curtsey and walk with a dress on and the rest of my costumes too. As you can see I had a lot of help being and liking to wear a dress on stage even more.

Now let me get back to the lady that did play the role Laurey Williams with the preforming arts group in our local theater. She made me wear a dress all the time when I had to meet with her and learn the instructions that she wanted to pass down to me so that I would learn my role as Laurey Williams and yes she wanted me to even wear the undergarments that I was to wear on stage as well. We even had a meeting whereby the two of us did meet just wearing our undergarments. This may should weird but there is a scene whereby I had to sing and dance just to the ladies in the play that where just wearing our undergarment fleshing up for the barn dance and the party that was to take place later on. Yes it was weird at first now dancing and singing in ladies undergarments in front of just the ladies and to the audience too. I was reinforced in my mind that yes I can do this, but most of all I would be relaxed and preform very great.

In matter of fact I was so relaxed and comfortable doing this now it would show up on opening night and our grade for our class too.

There was only one scene where I was a bit nervous that we did on opening night that I was real nervous and yes afraid to do and it was a number whereby I was singing this to the girls in the scene, for there was just girls in the scene only the number was, "Many A New Day". Now after I got over do this number I was so relaxed that being Laurey Williams that I did not even mind it when others did call me Laurey instead of my real name.

Now going back to being called Laurey even by my classmates did occur before that moment for even my very liberal feminist drama teacher and even the very liberal feminist principal even from time to time called me Laurey and that did not even bother me and I was used to it any ways.

In truth I actually had this as one of my main problems for if you know the play and . understand the fact that I even had to kiss another man who was Laurey's boyfriend and they do become husband and wife at the end of the play.

Okay the lady that did play the role Laurey Williams for the local preforming arts group came up with a plain to help me and the boy solve the problem of us kissing in the play on stage, and the plain was to have us meet and just talk about it.

Okay the boy and the girl that did play Aunt Eller and I did have a plain just to practice our lines and movements just said it this way. The boy that played Curly and I would have to just kiss and get it over with, but we had to make it look like the kisses where all real and just forget about it. This idea gave me the confidences to be a female and the three of us just agreed to convince me even more by saying just forget that I was a boy and for me to be a girl. So I just became a girl and I would no longer to be a boy any more while I was on stage.

So now you know I was able to be a girl and to in matter of fact just pretend to be a girl and to even convince everyone that by me being a girl and by having me play Laurey Williams we as a class was now even more convinced that we were going to get a very good grade and that would be a good thing.

Now as the opening night date does come closer and closer in my mind we as a class was very ready to preform and we would rehears and rehears over and over again did show up to how us as a class was going to perform on stage on opening night. Did we have opening night jitters? Yes we did but we did overcome those jitters.

Chapter Four

The Performance

When the curtain raises with the opening number I was waiting for my que to enter and start singing, and please note that yes I was nervous for about thirty seconds, but I got over that once I looked at the girl that played Aunt Eller and I saw her wink as to say do not be nervous. It was at that time I began to have fun and to real relax and I gained a lot of confidence that this was going to be a very good and great performance that we could do as a class.

The real thing that got me over being nervous was the fact was the time when the boy that played Curly put his arm around my waist and he began to hug me just a little bit, for I felt for a moment that he forgot that I was a boy and not a girl. Okay some of the things I did in the opening scene was to bat my eyes, smile, and yes be a flirt and tease just like a girl would do to a boy. When the girl that was playing the role Aunt Eller saw that I was flirting with the boy that was playing the role Curly she told me that that was very funny, and very cute of me to do. I told her as I can recall is well it was to help settle my nerves down and to help me relax. And yes I did enjoy doing that. In truth doing those things made it so much easier to do my performance too.

From going from scene to scene and wardrobe changes there was a place set up for me and just the adult ladies that were volunteering from the local preforming arts group along with the makeup lady helping me change into the different costumes that I had to change into my costumes and to make sure that everything was just right for the scenes that I was in. This was done for my safety and the fact that they wanted to make sure that I would not have any problems in getting into and out of my costumes too. Accurse I always wore the bloomers, tights, chemise, corset, petticoats, garters, and the western style high heels boots which was white in color in each and every scene. It was the different types of dresses and the wig that needed to be adjusted and fixed from time to time.

Here is some information that you should know about the play that would give you some idea what the play was all about. Laurey is a headstrong farm girl and the woman with whom both cowboy Curly and a farm hand Jud have fallen in love. When she plays hard-to-get with earnest Curly and instead accepts dangerous Jed's invitation to a box social, tension rise between the two men and capture the whole interest of the whole town. So now you can understand that I had to in truth teach myself how to be a flirt, and yes I had to learn this on my own, but us as a class did the history background and yes we knew this, but I was having trouble learning this because I was a very shy boy as you should recall and please note this too. Okay learning how to flirt with another boy as a boy as you can now understand is not what two boys do and it is very taboo to do, and even in 2016 not even acceptable for any male to do with another male.

It was in act one in this scene I did have a very hard time with even in all of our

rehearsals, for in the scene whereby I sing the song "Many of New Day" was a scene whereby the women in 1906 would go into the house and freshen up for the day. They would fix their clothing such as fix and tighten their corsets, freshen their hair, and even their makeup. Okay what was so hard for me to do and yes I would do it in all of our rehearsals great, but now I had an audience and the girls playing their roles in the undergarments of the times in 1906 to sing to as well. By the way after this scene in act one was over I had on my mind to even adlib just a little bit, but note I did it great and my very liberal feminist drama teacher commented this that I did a great job singing and doing this scene too she was well pleased.

The adlibbing that I did was to flirt more and to be more a female that was in love with her man. This man that Laurey was in love with was Curly. The girl that played Aunt Eller saw this and I no longer can recall the words that she used, but just to give you some idea of the type of words she used to me was "go girl". Then she would smile at me with a smile that meant things would be okay and we are on our way to get a great grade for our performance. I can even recall she even raised her eyebrows with that smile as to say yes I did it.

In the play there is a scene whereby Laurey would have a dream well she had bought a possession from a peddler that was to show her dreams and there is one problem here. Laurey saw a vision of the man that she was to marry, and her marriage. By the way yes I did learn how to do some ballet with my female western high heel boots on, and please not this was hard to do even in the play. But I was able to fake most of the dance steps seeing that I could not dance any ballet and this was my first time and only time even doing any ballet at all.

Now in the dream there was a fight that took place between Curly and Jud to see who would marry Laurey and there was a thing that happened in this fight, for Curly was killed by Jud and Laurey was forced to marry Jud. Laurey was even scared to marry Jud and she did not even want to marry Jud. I had to be a female or pretend to be a female in this dream scene too.

Well Laurey was forced to go to the box social by Jud, for he was the forceful type and very demanding type of man whereby his gal was to be his slave or worst. Now Laurey did not even want to go to the box social with Jud at all. So she does fight him off while she was in the buggy with him and somehow get away from him and heads to the box social by herself leaving Jud walk to the box social or to come up with a plain to kill Curly.

The real show down between Curly and Jud at the box social was the auctioning off the lunch baskets that was actioned off to see with man with be with gal, but Laurey and Aunt Eller had a plain to see if they could get Curly to outbid Jud for Laurey's lunch basket, for they were trying to raise money to build a school for the children.

Now seeing the Curly was dead broke and had no money in order to even bid on Laurey's lunch basket He had to sell everything that he owned to try and outbid Jud. Now Jud did have cash to outbid Curly. The bids came down to whereby Curly finely had to sell his horse. The final bit was fifty dollars and Curly did outbid Jud. Then Jud was every angry and went off to plot how he was going to kill Curly.

Seeing that Jud had ran off in a huff, and then in the mind of Laurey was a fear that Jud would take his revenge she met Curly and told him how she was afraid of Jud. So it was in this scene is what is call the "Curly's Marriage Proposal To Laurey" and you know what I even had the idea to just act like a lady and smile more with my eyes sparkling, but I even did more when he did propose to Laurey and I even added this to jump into his arm and this was our first kiss. Yes I gave the boy that did play the role Curly a big surprise and just kissed him on the lips, and hug him around the neck. My saying yes to Curly's marriage proposal in matter of fact even I forgot that I was a boy as well for just one simple moment, and I did feel like a female. Then we walked off that scene holding hands and I had my head on his shoulder with a huge smile on my face.

Next scene Jud came in and we did this scene different that the 1955 movie starring

Shirley Jones. We just acted out a fight between Jud and Curly and in the scene Jud was

accidently killed Jud in our scene too but not like it was in the 1955 version in the movie

Oklahoma. The fight was on the ground.

The wedding scene was next and the wedding dress that I had to wear was white with a

vail. In truth I did enjoy this scene, but instead of holding the wedding indoors like it was in the

movie we had it in an outdoor scene, but I made just one mistake. The mistake was I step

backwards and step on the back of the dress and I heard a very small rip. Well that was not so

bad, for I caught the mistake and corrected it fast before the dress even ripped.

It was at this point and the number came up whereby the musical was named

"Oklahoma" this would be our final dance, and to us in the class this was a number whereby we

did not want it to end.

Finally the play would end with Laurey and Curly riding off in the sunset in a buggy with

a fringe on top and with yellow wheels going on our honeymoon.

Okay I thought the play was over and it was for opening night, but the very last thing that

we had to do was to take a curtain call as they would do and take the final bow, but not so fast.

The curtain call is where the introduction us and the role that we played in the play. Well

the boy that played Curly and I was introduced last, then I was introduced last. While I was

giving my curtsey to the audience this was my biggest surprise. I had gotten a standing ovation

for my performance in the way I portrayed Laurey Williams. Yes I can recall I had tears in my

eyes for this was the very first time I had standing ovation.

The other surprises to the class was there was a critic for the local newspaper that did

. review the play and our performance, and gave us a review of the performance and how each

and every one of did. The critic even thought that I was a female by the way and said my

performance was great for a girl my age. Okay I was blushing for I did just what I was to do and

pass as a girl, and I thought that my punishment was over, but no, for the play was held over for

one more year. Oh no Now I had to be a girl for a year was now on my mind, and yes I was mad

for that. I took it in stride by the way and did it.

Now as you can recall that the local preforming arts group did help us a long, and the

lady that did play the very same role as I did in the play asked me to play at least one time on

their stage. She was so impressed by the way I preformed is the reason why she wanted me to try

it just one time. So I did it, and the very same thing happen as I had to take the curtain call. I was

given another standing ovation this time too.

The lady that did play this role told me that she was very proud of me in both

performances by saying this or something like this as I can recall. She said that if she did not

know that I was a boy she even thought that I was a girl with a lot of talent too.

Now my mother got to keep all my dresses and other parts of my costumes I wore and

there were pictures taken she had all of that locked in a truck, for she loved to keep things like

this as memories to my childhood.

I have never wore any female clothing since this performance that we had to do in 1968

in the musical paly Oklahoma, for this was the very last time I would do this.

Yes there are more secrets that I could tell you, but I just gave you a very good glimpse into what I had to go through as a boy when I was a boy and yes a very shy boy being dressed as a girl from time to time. I also gave you an insight to how I was feeling and how I felt as a boy then as a girl too.

The End